52 Bodybuilder Breakfast Meals High In Protein:

Increase Muscle Fast Without Pills, Protein Supplements, or Protein Bars

By

Joseph Correa

Certified Sports Nutritionist

COPYRIGHT

© 2016 Correa Media Group

All rights reserved

Reproduction or translation of any part of this work beyond that permitted by section 107 or 108 of the 1976 United States Copyright Act without the permission of the copyright owner is unlawful.

This publication is designed to provide accurate and authoritative information in regard to the subject matter covered. It is sold with the understanding that neither the author nor the publisher is engaged in rendering medical advice. If medical advice or assistance is needed, consult with a doctor. This book is considered a guide and should not be used in any way detrimental to your health. Consult with a physician before starting this nutritional plan to make sure it's right for you.

ACKNOWLEDGEMENTS

The realization and success of this book could not have been possible without my family.

52 Bodybuilder Breakfast Meals High In Protein:

Increase Muscle Fast Without Pills, Protein Supplements, or Protein Bars

By

Joseph Correa

Certified Sports Nutritionist

CONTENTS

Copyright

Acknowledgements

About The Author

Introduction

52 Bodybuilder Breakfast Meals High In Protein

Other Great Titles by This Author

ABOUT THE AUTHOR

As a certified sports nutritionist and professional athlete, I firmly believe that proper nutrition will help you reach your goals faster and effectively. My knowledge and experience has helped me live healthier throughout the years and which I have shared with family and friends. The more you know about eating and drinking healthier, the sooner you will want to change your life and eating habits.

Being successful in controlling your weight is important as it will improve all aspects of your life.

Nutrition is a key part in the process of getting in better shape and that's what this book is all about.

INTRODUCTION

52 Bodybuilder Breakfast Meals High In Protein will help you increase the amount of protein you consume per day to help increase muscle mass. These meals will help increase muscle in an organized manner by adding large healthy portions of protein to your diet. Being too busy to eat right can sometimes become a problem and that's why this book will save you time and help nourish your body to achieve the goals you want. Make sure you know what you're eating by preparing it yourself or having someone prepare it for you.

This book will help you to:

-Gain muscle fast naturally at breakfast time.

-Improve muscle recovery.

-Have more energy.

-Naturally accelerate Your Metabolism to build more muscle.

-Improve your digestive system.

Joseph Correa is a certified sports nutritionist and a professional athlete.

52 Bodybuilder Breakfast Meals High In Protein

1. Avocado eggs

Ingredients:

3 medium ripe avocados, cut in half

6 eggs

3 tbsp of olive oil

2 tsp of dried rosemary

salt and pepper to taste

Preparation:

Preheat oven to 350 degrees. Cut avocado in half and remove the flesh from the center. Place one egg in each avocado half and sprinkle with rosemary, salt and pepper. Grease the baking pan with olive oil and place the avocados. You want to use a small baking pan so your avocados can fit tightly. Place in the oven for about 15-20 minutes.

Nutritional values per 100g:

Carbohydrates 4.8g

Sugar 3.1g

Protein 29 g

Total fat 11.7g

Sodium 127 mg

Potassium 239mg

Calcium 2.9mg

Iron 2.16mg

Vitamins (vitamin A; B-6; B-12; C; D; D2; D3; K; Riboflavin; Niacin; Thiamin; K)

Calories 213

2. Quinoa smoothie

Ingredients:

1 cup of quinoa, cooked

1 banana

½ cup of strawberries

1 cup of low fat yogurt

1 cup of skim milk

1 tsp of ground vanilla sticks

1 tsp of honey

Preparation:

Combine the ingredients in a blender and mix for few minutes, until smooth mixture. Allow it to cool in the refrigerator for a while.

Nutritional values per one cup:

Carbohydrates 6.2g

Sugar 5.4g

Protein 29.7 g

Total fat 12.2g

Sodium 123 mg

Potassium 224mg

Calcium 4.9mg

Iron 2.18mg

Vitamins (vitamin A; B-6; B-12; C; D; D2; D3; K; Riboflavin; Niacin; Thiamin; K)

Calories 84

3. Peanut butter oats

Ingredients:

1 cup of oats, cooked

1 cup of unsweetened almond milk

2 tbsp of organic peanut butter

1 tbsp of strawberry syrup

1 tsp of cinnamon

Preparation:

Place the ingredients in a bowl and stir well until you get a nice, smooth mixture. If necessary, add some water. Pour this mixture in a tall glasses and leave in the refrigerator overnight.

Nutritional values per 100g:

Carbohydrates 7.6g

Sugar 5.9g

Protein 26 g

Total fat 11.1g

Sodium 124.5 mg

Potassium 201mg

Calcium 2.4mg

Iron 2mg

Vitamins (vitamin A; B-6; B-12; C; D; D2; D3; K; Riboflavin; Niacin; Thiamin; K)

Calories 117

4. Egg and cheese sandwich

Ingredients:

4 eggs

1 cup of cottage cheese

1 tsp of dried parsley

8 thin slices of whole grain bread

salt to taste

Preparation:

Boil the eggs for 10 minutes. Allow to cool and peel them. Cut into thin slices – about 5-6 slices of each egg. Layer 1 tbsp of low-fat cottage cheese on top of the bread and top with the egg, sliced.

Nutritional values per 100g:

Carbohydrates 9.7g

Sugar 7.1g

Protein 24g

Total fat 9g

Sodium 117mg

Potassium 115mg

Calcium 2.6mg

Iron 2.34mg

Vitamins (vitamin A; B-6; B-12; C; D; D2; D3; K; Riboflavin; Niacin; Thiamin; K)

Calories 209

5. Cottage cheese with berries

Ingredients:

1 cup of cottage cheese

1 cup of wild berries

½ cup of low fat cream

2 egg whites

1 tbsp of honey

1 tsp of brown sugar

Preparation:

Combine the ingredients in a large bowl. Beat well with a fork. Put it in a freezer for about 30 minutes. This creamy mixture goes perfectly with a whole grain toast.

Nutritional values per 100g:

Carbohydrates 5.1g

Sugar 4.7g

Protein 19 g

Total fat 9.8g

Sodium 101 mg

Potassium 112mg

Calcium 5.45mg

Iron 1.6mg

Vitamins (vitamin A; B-6; B-12; C; D; D2; D3; K; Riboflavin; Niacin; Thiamin; K)

Calories 91

6. Chia seeds with Greek yogurt

Ingredients:

1 cup of Greek yogurt

3 tbsp of chia seeds

1 tsp of ground almonds

1 tbsp of honey

Preparation:

Chia seeds are very popular because of their nutritional values. There is a reason why they're called 'superfood'. Add this high quality ingredient into your regular Greek yogurt and you will have a great meal full of proteins and other valuable ingredients.

For this easy recipe, combine 3 tbsp of chia seeds with 1 cup of Greek yogurt, 1 tsp of ground almonds and 1 tbsp of honey. Use a fork or an electric mixer to get a smooth mixture. Allow it to cool in the refrigerator.

Nutritional values per 100g:

Carbohydrates 3.1g

Sugar 2.12g

Protein 9.7 g

Total fat 4.8g

Sodium 73mg

Potassium 99mg

Calcium 3.9mg

Iron 0.16mg

Vitamins (vitamin A; B-6; B-12; K; Riboflavin; Niacin;)

Calories 89

7. Bacon and spinach omelet

Ingredients:

3 eggs

1 cup of fresh spinach

5 thin slices of bacon

¼ cup of milk

1 tbsp of olive oil

1/8 tsp of ground red pepper

¼ tsp of salt

Preparation:

Grease the frying pan with olive oil. Heat up over to medium-high heat. Meanwhile, whisk together eggs, spinach and milk. Pour into pan and stir for 3-4 minutes. Add bacon, ground pepper and salt. Turn off heat, but keep the pan on burner until ham is heated.

Nutritional values per 100g:

Carbohydrates 5.3g

Sugar 3.19g

Protein 28.9 g

Total fat 11.8g

Sodium 112 mg

Potassium 139mg

Calcium 1.9mg

Iron 1.18mg

Vitamins (B-6; B-12; D)

Calories 213

8. Eggplant casserole

Ingredients:

2 large eggplants

1 cup of minced meat

1 onion

2 tbsp of olive oil

¼ tsp of pepper

2 tomatoes

1 tbsp of dried parsley

4 eggs

3 tbsp of bread crumbs

1 cup of skim milk

½ cup of low fat cream

Preparation:

Grease the baking pan with olive oil. Preheat the oven at 350 degrees. Peel the eggplants and cut them lengthwise into thin slices. Layer eggplant slices in a baking pan. Peel and cut the onion and tomatoes into thin slices. Make another layer in a baking pan. Spread the meat on top. Now combine bread crumbs with milk, eggs, low fat cream, parsley and pepper in a large bowl. Whisk well until smooth mixture. Pour this mixture on top of your casserole and bake for about 20 minutes. Cut into 6 equal pieces.

Nutritional values per 100g:

Carbohydrates 12.7g

Sugar 9.1g

Protein 29.3 g

Total fat 11g

Sodium 237 mg

Potassium 289mg

Calcium 5.9mg

Iron 4.2mg

Vitamins (vitamin A; B-6; B-12; C; D; D2; D3; K; Riboflavin; Niacin; Thiamin; K)

Calories 227

9. Fried egg whites with cottage cheese

Ingredients:

4 eggs

1 cup of cottage cheese

¼ cup of skim milk

1 tbsp of olive oil

salt to taste

Preparation:

Remove the egg whites from yolks. Grease the frying pan with olive oil. Heat up over to medium-high heat. Whisk together egg whites, cottage cheese and milk. Add some salt to taste. Fry for 3-4 minutes, stirring constantly.

Nutritional values per 100g:

Carbohydrates 2.1g

Sugar 2g

Protein 17.8g

Total fat 9.8g

Sodium 137 mg

Potassium 109mg

Calcium 5.3mg

Iron 1.16mg

Vitamins (vitamin A; B-6; B-12; D; D2; D3)

Calories 179

10. Crunchy almond delight

Ingredients:

1 cup of Greek yogurt

½ cup of frozen blueberries

¼ cup of whole almonds

1 tbsp of honey

Preparation:

Combine the ingredients in a blender and mix for 30 seconds. Pour the mixture into tall glass and leave in the freezer for about an hour.

Nutritional values per one cup:

Carbohydrates 7.7g

Sugar 5.1g

Protein 14 g

Total fat 6.8g

Sodium 112 mg

Potassium 129mg

Calcium 3.9mg

Iron 1.12mg

Vitamins (vitamin A; B-6; B-12;D; D2; D3; K)

Calories 87

11. Eggplant French toast

Ingredients:

1 large eggplant

3 eggs

¼ tsp of sea salt

1 tbsp of coconut oil

½ tsp of cinnamon

Preparation:

Peel eggplant and cut into slices. Sprinkle salt on each side of eggplant. Allow it to rest for few minutes. Meanwhile, mix eggs with cinnamon in a large bowl. Melt coconut oil in frying pan on medium heat.

Put your eggplant slices in egg mixture. Make few holes with a knife to allow the mixture to permeate the eggplant. Fry it until golden brown color, on each side. Serve your 'French toast' warm.

Nutritional values per 100g:

Carbohydrates 9.4g

Sugar 6.3g

Protein 19 g

Total fat 10.8g

Sodium 167 mg

Potassium 234mg

Calcium 3.3mg

Iron 2.44mg

Vitamins (vitamin A; B-6; B-12; C; D; D2; D3; K; Riboflavin; Niacin; Thiamin; K)

Calories 187

12. Feta and eggs toast

Ingredients:

4 slices of whole grain bread

3 eggs

1 cup of baby spinach, chopped

½ cup of feta cheese

2 tbsp of extra virgin olive oil

Preparation:

Beat the eggs with a fork in a bowl. Cut feta cheese into small cubes and add them to the bowl. Grease the frying pan with olive oil. Heat up over to medium-high heat and fry baby spinach for several minutes, stirring constantly. Add egg and feta mixture and fry for several more minutes.

Put the bread in the toaster for 2 minutes. Serve with egg, feta and spinach mixture.

Nutritional values per 100g:

Carbohydrates 13.7g

Sugar 7.1g

Protein 26.7 g

Total fat 11.8g

Sodium 141 mg

Potassium 223mg

Calcium 4.5mg

Iron 2.54mg

Vitamins (vitamin A; B-6; B-12; C; D; D2; D3; K; Riboflavin; Niacin; Thiamin; K)

Calories 197

13. Greek yogurt protein shake

Ingredients:

3 cups of Greek yogurt

3 egg whites

1 cup of fresh apple juice

½ cup of frozen mango, chopped

½ cup of frozen pineapple, chopped

1 tbsp of honey

1 tbsp of natural orange extract

Preparation:

Combine the ingredients in a blender and mix for 30-40 seconds. Serve cold.

Nutritional values per one cup:

Carbohydrates 15.7g

Sugar 11.13g

Protein 29 g

Total fat 7.8g

Sodium 196 mg

Potassium 289mg

Calcium 5.35mg

Iron 6.15mg

Vitamins (vitamin A; B-6; B-12; C; D; D2; D3; K; Riboflavin; Niacin; Thiamin; K)

Calories 165

14. Wild berries smoothie

Ingredients:

1 cup of skim milk

½ cup of water

3 egg whites

½ cup of mixed wild berries, frozen

1 banana

½ cup of ice cubes

1 tbsp of honey

½ tsp of cinnamon

Preparation:

Combine the ingredients in a blender for few minutes. Allow it to cool in the refrigerator for about an hour.

Nutritional values per one cup:

Carbohydrates 9.7g

Sugar 8.1g

Protein 24 g

Total fat 4.8g

Sodium 187 mg

Potassium 267mg

Calcium 4.5mg

Iron 2.45mg

Vitamins (vitamin A; B-6; B-12; C; D; D2; D3; K; Riboflavin; Niacin; Thiamin; K)

Calories 143

15. Cottage cheese and banana pancakes

Ingredients:

1 cup of sliced banana

½ cup of rice flower

½ cup of skim milk

½ cup of almond milk

3 tbsp of brown sugar

1 tsp of vanilla extract

1 egg

½ cup of low fat cream

non-fat cooking spray

Preparation:

Combine banana slices, flour, skim milk and almond milk in a bowl and mix with an electric mixer until smooth mixture. Cover it and let it stand for 15 minutes.

In another bowl, mix the cream with sugar vanilla extract and egg. Beat well with a fork, or even better with an electric mixer. You want to get a foamy mixture. Set aside.

Sprinkle some non-fat cooking spray on a frying pen. Use ¼ cup of banana mixture to make one pancake. Fry your pancakes for about 2-3 minutes on each side. This mixture should give you 8 pancakes.

Spread 1 tbsp of cheese mixture over each pancake and serve.

Nutritional values per 100g:

Carbohydrates 22.4g

Sugar 19.1g

Protein 24 g

Total fat 17.8g

Sodium 194 mg

Potassium 297mg

Calcium 3.9mg

Iron 2.876mg

Vitamins (vitamin A; B-6; B-12; C; D; D2; D3; K)

Calories 143

16. Spinach omelet

Ingredients:

4 eggs

1 cup of baby spinach leaves, chopped

1 tbsp of onion powder

¼ tsp of ground red pepper

¼ tsp of sea salt

1 tbsp of Parmesan cheese

1 tbsp of olive oil

Preparation:

Beat the eggs with a fork, in a large bowl. Add baby spinach and Parmesan cheese. Mix well. Season with onion powder, red pepper and sea salt.

Heat upIn a bowl, beat the eggs, and stir in the baby spinach and Parmesan cheese. Season with onion powder, nutmeg, salt, and pepper.

Heat up the olive oil over a medium heat. Add egg mixture and fry for 2-3 minutes.

Nutritional values per 100g:

Carbohydrates 7.2g

Sugar 5.1g

Protein 29.6 g

Total fat 6.8g

Sodium 167 mg

Potassium 249mg

Calcium 4.9mg

Iron 5.16mg

Vitamins (vitamin A; B-6; B-12; C; D; D2; D3; K; Riboflavin; Niacin; Thiamin; K)

Calories 190

17. Mocha protein smoothie

Ingredients:

1 cup of ice cubes

1 tbsp of grated dark chocolate (80% of cocoa)

1 tbsp of cocoa

½ cup of almond milk

1 cup of skim milk

3 egg whites

1 tsp of instant mocha

Preparation:

Mix ice, dark chocolate, cocoa, almond milk and instant mocha and blend thoroughly. Pour in tall glasses and serve cold.

Nutritional values per one cup:

Carbohydrates 4.7g

Sugar 3.1g

Protein 17.6 g

Total fat 8.8g

Sodium 101mg

Potassium 139mg

Calcium 3.9mg

Iron 1.6mg

Vitamins (vitamin A; B-6; B-12; D; D2)

Calories 79

18. Sweet potatoes with egg whites

Ingredients:

4 medium sweet potatoes, peeled

6 eggs

2 medium onions, peeled

1 tbsp of ground garlic

2 tbsp of olive oil

½ tsp of sea salt

¼ tsp of ground pepper

Preparation:

Preheat your oven to 350 degrees. Spread the olive oil over a medium sized baking sheet. Place the potatoes on a baking sheet. Bake for about 40 minutes. Remove from the oven and allow it to cool for a while. Lover the oven heat to 200 degrees.

Meanwhile, chop the onions into small pieces. Separate egg whites from yolks. Cut the potatoes into thick slices and place them in a bowl. Add chopped onions, egg whites, ground garlic, sea salt and pepper. Mix well.

Spread this mixture over a baking sheet and bake for another 15-20 minutes.

Nutritional values per 100g:

Carbohydrates 16.7g

Sugar 9.1g

Protein 19 g

Total fat 11.8g

Sodium 127 mg

Potassium 114mg

Calcium 1.3mg

Iron 2.12mg

Vitamins (vitamin A; B-6; D; D2; D3; K; Riboflavin; Niacin; Thiamin)

Calories 204

19. Protein burritos

Ingredients:

1 cup of cooked green beans

1 pound of lean ground beef

1 cup of cottage cheese

½ cup of chopped onions

1 tsp of ground red pepper

1 tsp of chili powder

6 whole grain tortillas

Preparation:

Cook up the meat and rinse it. Chop it into bite size pieces and put it back in the pan. Add ground red pepper, chili powder and onions. Stir well for 15 minutes. Remove from the heat.

Combine cottage cheese with green beans in a blender. Mix well for 30 seconds. Add the cheese mixture to the meat. Divide this mixture into 6 equal pieces and spread over tortillas. Wrap and serve.

Nutritional values per 100g:

Carbohydrates 21g

Sugar 15.1g

Protein 32.4 g

Total fat 19.8g

Sodium 337 mg

Potassium 223mg

Calcium 2.4mg

Iron 2.42mg

Vitamins (vitamin A; B-6; B-12; C; D; D2; D3; K; Riboflavin; Niacin; Thiamin; K)

Calories 264

20. Almond parfait

Ingredients:

2 tbsp of grated dark chocolate (80% of cocoa)

2 cups of skim milk

2 tbsp of low fat cream

1 whole egg

2 egg whites

1 tbsp of honey

½ cup of toasted almonds

Preparation:

Gently warm the skim milk over a low temperature. Add cream and stir well. You don't want it to boil! Remove from the heat and add chocolate. Stir until the chocolate melts. Set side and allow it to cool for a while. Now add egg and egg whites, honey and almonds. Stir well for several minutes and pour into tall glasses. Freeze overnight and serve.

Nutritional values per 1 cup:

Carbohydrates 10.7g

Sugar 7.5g

Protein 23 g

Total fat 9.8g

Sodium 133 mg

Potassium 211mg

Calcium 5.9mg

Iron 2.34mg

Vitamins (vitamin A; B-6; B-12; C; D; D2; D3; K)

Calories 89

21. Cranberry oatmeal

Ingredients:

1 cup of fresh cranberries

2 cups of rolled oats

1 tbsp of pumpkin seeds

1 medium apple, cut into slices

1 cup of low fat yogurt

3 egg whites

½ cup of maple syrup

Preparation:

Preheat the oven to 350 degrees. Spread the pumpkin seeds in a baking sheet and toast for about 5-6 minutes. You want a nice lightly brown color.

Boil the cranberries over a high temperature. Cook until they burst. Add the oats, egg whites and apple slices and stir well. Cook for another 7 minutes, or until the oats are cooked. Stir in the pumpkin seeds. Remove from the heat and let it stand for 10 minutes. Serve cold with the yogurt and maple syrup.

Nutritional values per 100g:

Carbohydrates 14.7g

Sugar 10.1g

Protein 16 g

Total fat 11.8g

Sodium 187 mg

Potassium 278mg

Calcium 5.56mg

Iron 1.34mg

Vitamins (vitamin A; B-6; B-12; C; D; D2; D3; K; Riboflavin; Niacin; Thiamin; K)

Calories 121

22. Scrambled eggs with tumeric

Ingredients:

3 eggs

3 egg whites

1 tbsp of olive oil

1 tsp of ground tumeric

salt and pepper to taste

Preparation:

Grease the frying pan with olive oil. Heat up over to medium-high heat. Meanwhile, whisk together eggs, egg whites and tumeric. Add some salt and pepper to taste and fry for few minutes.

Nutritional values per 100g:

Carbohydrates 2.7g

Sugar 1.3g

Protein 19 g

Total fat 9.8g

Sodium 111 mg

Potassium 122mg

Calcium 1.23mg

Iron 0.16mg

Vitamins (vitamin A; B-6; B-12; C; D)

Calories 213

23. Mediterranean quick snacks

Ingredients:

3/4 cup of ground almonds

1/4 cup of grated coconut

3/4 cup of goji berries

1 cup of coconut milk

½ glass of water

1 tsp of vanilla extract

1 tsp of grated orange peel

1 tsp of chili powder

3 tbsp of grated dark chocolate with 85% of cocoa

Preparation:

First you need to mix the grated orange peel with chili, vanilla extract and coconut milk. Cook on a low temperature for 10-15 minutes. Allow it to cool. Meanwhile, mix the almonds, grated coconut, goji berries and water in a blender for few minutes. Add the cooled mixture of chili, vanilla extract, orange peel and coconut milk and mix for another 1-2 minutes. Pour the mixture into round molds and sprinkle with dark chocolate on top. Let it stand in the refrigerator for few hours.

Nutritional values per 100g:

Carbohydrates 14.5g

Sugar 2.61g

Protein 13.5g

Total fat 16.6 g

Sodium 49,5mg

Potassium 331mg

Calcium 121,8mg

Iron 37.6mg

Vitamins (Vitamin C; B-6; B-12; A-RAE; D; D-D2+D3; K-phylloquinone; Thianin; Riboflavin; Niacin)

Calories 248 kcal

24. Protein vanilla pancakes

Ingredients:

4 eggs

2 cups of skim milk

½ cup of rice flour

2 tbsp of brown sugar

½ tsp of salt salt

1 tsp of baking soda

½ tsp of vanilla extract

Preparation:

Combine eggs, milk, flour, salt, baking soda and vanilla in a medium bowl. Mix well with electric mixer.

Use ¼ cup of this mixture to make one pancake. Fry on a medium temperature until golden brown on each side. Serve warm.

Nutritional values per 100g:

Carbohydrates 4.7g

Sugar 4.1g

Protein 29 g

Total fat 11.8g

Sodium 137 mg

Potassium 239mg

Calcium 2.9mg

Iron 2.16mg

Vitamins (vitamin A; B-6; B-12; C; D; D2; D3; K; Riboflavin; Niacin; Thiamin; K)

Calories 213

25. Blueberry protein shake

Ingredients:

1 cup of frozen blueberries

1 cup of skim milk

3 egg whites

1 cup of water

1 tbsp of brown sugar

½ cup of walnuts

Preparation:

Combine the ingredients in a blender and mix for 30-40 seconds.

Serve cold.

Nutritional values per one cup:

Carbohydrates 8.7g

Sugar 8.1g

Protein 19 g

Total fat 9.8g

Sodium 127 mg

Potassium 139mg

Calcium 1.22mg

Iron 2.16mg

Vitamins (vitamin A; B-6; B-12; C; D; D2)

Calories 91

26. Egg and avocado puree

Ingredients:

4 eggs

1 cup of skim milk

½ avocado

Preparation:

Hard boil your eggs. Remove from the heat and allow it to cool. Peel and cut the eggs. Add a pinch of salt and leave in the refrigerator for about 30 minutes. Place in a blender. Cut avocado into small pieces and add to the blender. Add milk and blend for 30 minutes. This puree should be eaten right away.

Nutritional values per 100g:

Carbohydrates 8.7g

Sugar 5.1g

Protein 17 g

Total fat 7.8g

Sodium 112 mg

Potassium 101mg

Calcium 3.4mg

Iron 0.23mg

Vitamins (vitamin A; B-6; B-12; C; D; D2; D3)

Calories 176

27. Mixed nuts protein shake

Ingredients:

1 tsp of grated almonds

1 tsp of grated walnuts

1 tsp of grated hazelnuts

1 tsp of grated macadamia nuts

1 glass of fresh orange juice

1 tbsp of agave syrup

1 tbsp of non fat orange ice cream

1 handful of ice cubes

Preparation:

Mix the ingredients in a blender for 30-40 seconds.

Nutritional values for 1 glass:

Carbohydrates 15.19g

Sugar 11.23g

Protein 9.85g

Total fat 6.64g

Sodium 115mg

Potassium 309.6mg

Calcium 121mg

Iron 5.03mg

Vitamins (Vitamin C total ascorbic acid; B-6; B-12; Folate-DFE; A-RAE; A-IU; E-alpha-tocopherol; D; D-D2+D3; K-phylloquinone; Thianin; Riboflavin; Niacin)

Calories 98.3

28. Walnut and strawberries salad

Ingredients:

½ cup of ground walnuts

2 cups of fresh strawberries

1 tbsp of strawberry syrup

2 tbsp of non fat cream

1 tbsp of brown sugar

Preparation:

Wash and cut the strawberries into small pieces. Mix with ground walnuts in a bowl. In a separate bowl, combine strawberry syrup, non fat cream and brown sugar. Beat well with a fork and use to top the salad.

Nutritional values per 100g:

Carbohydrates 9.7g

Sugar 8.1g

Protein 17 g

Total fat 9.8g

Sodium 137 mg

Potassium 234mg

Calcium 3.4mg

Iron 3.16mg

Vitamins (vitamin A; B-6; B-12; C; D; D2; D3; K; Riboflavin; Niacin; Thiamin; K)

Calories 176

29. Ginger omelet

Ingredients:

3 eggs

2 tbsp of olive oil

1 tsp of grated ginger

1/5 tsp of pepper

¼ tsp of sea salt

Preparation:

Beat the eggs with a fork. Add ginger and pepper. Mix well and fry in olive oil for few minutes. Serve warm. Season with sea salt.

Nutritional values per 100g:

Carbohydrates 0.9g

Sugar 0.45g

Protein 12g

Total fat 12.4g

Sodium 156mg

Potassium 117.5mg

Calcium 4.4mg

Iron 7.37mg

Vitamins (vitamin A; B-6; D; D2; D3)

Calories 156

30. Scrambled eggs with green pepper

Ingredients:

2 whole eggs

2 egg whites

2 small green peppers, chopped

¼ tsp of red pepper

¼ tsp of sea salt

1 tbsp of olive oil

Preparation:

Beat the eggs and egg whites with a fork. Season the eggs with red pepper and sea salt.

Heat up the olive oil over to medium-high heat and fry the chopped green peppers for about 10 minutes. Add eggs, stir well and fry for another 3 minutes. Remove from the heat and serve.

Nutritional values per 100g:

Carbohydrates 10.7g

Sugar 8.1g

Protein 17g

Total fat 8.8g

Sodium 134 mg

Potassium 253mg

Calcium 2.5mg

Iron 1.34mg

Vitamins (vitamin A; B-6; B-12; C; D; D2; D3)

Calories 175

31. Almond protein shake

Ingredients:

1 cup of almond milk

1 cup of skim milk

3 egg whites

1 tsp of cinnamon

1 cup of strawberries

½ cup of ground almonds

1 tsp of almond extract

Preparadion:

Mix the ingredients in a blender for about 30-40 seconds. Serve cold.

Nutritional values per 1 cup:

Carbohydrates 9.7g

Sugar 5.1g

Protein 21 g

Total fat 7.8g

Sodium 111 mg

Potassium 132mg

Calcium 1.2mg

Iron 4.16mg

Vitamins (vitamin A; B-6; B-12; C; D; D2; D3; K; Riboflavin; Niacin; Thiamin; K)

Calories 98

32. Apple muesli with chia seeds

Ingredients:

½ cup of dried chia seeds

2 large apples

3 tbsp of flax seeds

3 tbsp of honey

1 ¼ cups of coconut water

1 ¼ cups of plain yogurt

1 cup of rolled oats

2 tablespoons of mint leaves

Himalayan crystal salt, to taste

Preparation:

Wash and peel the apples. Cut them into bite size pieces and place in a large bowl. Add yogurt, chia seeds, flax seeds, rolled oats, mint and coconut water in the bowl and stir well. Leave the mixture in the fridge overnight.

Add salt and honey before serving.

Nutritional values per 100g:

Carbohydrates 10.7g

Sugar 8.1g

Protein 18 g

Total fat 11.8g

Sodium 137 mg

Potassium 239mg

Calcium 2.9mg

Iron 2.16mg

Vitamins (vitamin A; B-6; B-12; C; D; D2; D3; K; Riboflavin; Niacin; Thiamin; K)

Calories 198

33. Walnut bread with honey

Ingredients:

1 tbsp of honey

½ cup of ground walnuts

2 cups of almond flour

1 tbsp of vanilla extract

3 large eggs

5 egg whites

½ tsp of sea salt

1 teaspoon of baking soda

2 tbsp of coconut oil

Preparation:

Put the honey, eggs, egg whites, walnuts and vanilla extract in the food processor and mix well for 40 seconds.

Pour the mixture in a bowl and add flour, baking soda and salt. Stir well with a fork or even better with an electric stick mixer to get a smooth dough.

Pour the coconut oil over a baking sheet. Preheat the oven to 250 degrees. It takes about 40 minutes for bread to start rising. When it does, remove it from the oven and let it stand for at least 2 hours before eating.

This bread is high in proteins and very good alternative to your regular bread.

Nutritional values per 100g:

Carbohydrates 31g

Sugar 17g

Protein 25g

Total fat 11.8g

Sodium 177 mg

Potassium 322mg

Calcium 4.9mg

Iron 5.16mg

Vitamins (vitamin A; B-6; B-12; C; D; D2; D3; K; Riboflavin; Niacin; Thiamin; K)

Calories 312

34. Almond pancakes

Ingredients:

1 cup of oats

½ cup of minced almonds

2 egg whites

1 cup of milk

½ cup of water

salt

cinnamon to taste

1 tbsp of coconut oil

Preparation:

Make a smooth dough with oats, almonds, egg whites, salt and water, using an electric mixer. Add some cinnamon to taste and fry over a medium heat for about 3-4 minutes on each side. These pancakes are perfect with strawberry syrup on top.

Nutritional values per 100g:

Carbohydrates 21.3g

Sugar 19g

Protein 23g

Total fat 16.6g

Sodium 193.5mg

Potassium 278mg

Calcium 3.4mg

Iron 2.8mg

Vitamins (vitamin A; B-6; B-12; C; D; D2; D3; K)

Calories 148

35. Chia seeds & fruit shake

Ingredients:

1 small apple

1 small orange

½ glass of water

1 tbsp of minced chia seeds

1 tsp of chopped almonds

3 egg whites

2 tbsp of non fat cream

½ cup of ice cubes

Preparation:

Combine the ingredients in a blender for 30-40 seconds. Drink cold.

Nutritional values per 1 cup:

Carbohydrates 8g

Sugar 4.9g

Protein 10.2g

Total fat 2.67g

Sodium 74mg

Potassium 312.9mg

Calcium 79mg

Iron 1.88mg

Vitamins (Vitamin B-6; B-12; D; D-D2+D3)

Calories 56

36. Hazelnuts and strawberries shake

Ingredients:

1 cup of strawberries

1 glass of non-fat milk

¼ cup of ground hazelnuts

1 tbsp of low fat cream

1 tbsp of honey

1 tsp of brown sugar

3 egg whites

Preparation:

Remove the egg whites from yolks. Combine the ingredients in a blender for 30-40 seconds.

Nutritional values per 1 cup:

Carbohydrates 9.76g

Sugar 6.9g

Protein 11g

Total fat 1.9g

Sodium 98mg

Potassium 212.9mg

Calcium 56mg

Iron 1.87mg

Vitamins (Vitamin B-6; B-12; D; D-D2+D3)

Calories 67

37. Eggs with fried vegetables and chia seeds

Ingredients:

2 eggs

3 egg whites

1 small onion

1 small carrot

1 small tomato

2 medium red peppers

1 tbsp of ground chia seeds

salt

1 tbsp of olive oil

Preparation:

Wash and pat dry the vegetables using a kitchen paper. Cut into slices or strips. Heat up the olive oil over a medium temperature and fry the vegetables for about 10 minutes, stirring constantly. Add chia seeds and mix well. You want to wait until the vegetables soften and add eggs. Fry for another 2-3 minutes. Remove from the heat and serve.

Nutritional values per 100g:

Carbohydrates 12g

Sugar 9.9g

Protein 19.4g

Total fat 11.9g

Sodium 174mg

Potassium 212.9mg

Calcium 79mg

Iron 3.1mg

Vitamins (Vitamin B-6; B-12; D; D-D2+D3)

Calories 156

38. Breakfast mousse

Ingredients:

½ cup of blueberries

¼ cup of strawberries

½ glass of skim milk

1 tbsp of low fat cream

3 egg whites

1 tbsp of vanilla extract

cinnamon to taste

Preparation:

Beat the egg whites, low fat cream and skim milk with a fork. It will take about 5 minutes to get a nice, smooth mousse. Pour this mousse in a blender, add blueberries, strawberries and mix for 20 seconds. Add some cinnamon and vanilla extract before serving.

Nutritional values per 1 cup:

Carbohydrates 8.9g

Sugar 5.9g

Protein 12.3g

Total fat 1.7g

Sodium 114mg

Potassium 212mg

Calcium 1.34mg

Iron 1.34mg

Vitamins (Vitamin B-6; B-12; D; D-D2+D3)

Calories 76

39. Vanilla shake

Ingredients:

1 glass of skim milk

1 tsp of vanilla extract

1 tbsp of minced chia seeds

4 egg whites

1 tbsp of non fat cream

cinnamon

1 tsp of sugar

Preparation:

Mix well the ingredients in a blender for 30 seconds. Serve cold.

Nutritional values per 1 cup:

Carbohydrates 12.2g

Sugar 7.5g

Protein 14g

Total fat 5.65g

Sodium 121mg

Potassium 231.4mg

Calcium 22mg

Iron 1.9mg

Vitamins (Vitamin C total ascorbic acid; B-6; B-12; Folate-DFE; A-RAE; A-IU; D; D-D2+D3; K-phylloquinone; Thianin; Riboflavin; Niacin)

Calories 80

40. Coconut milk pancakes with strawberries

Ingredients:

1 glass of coconut milk

3 egg whites

1 glass of water

salt

1 cup of buckwheat flour

½ cup of ground walnuts

½ cup of strawberries

olive oil for frying

Preparation:

Mix well coconut milk, egg whites and water in a large bowl. Add flour and salt and mix well with a stick blender, to get a smooth dough. Add ground walnuts. Heat up the olive oil over a medium temperature. Make a pancakes with ¼ cup of dough. Fry in hot oil and top with strawberries.

Nutritional values per 100g:

Carbohydrates 23.2g

Sugar 18g

Protein 26 g

Total fat 15.3g

Sodium 172 mg

Potassium 247mg

Calcium 3.6mg

Iron 2.36mg

Vitamins (vitamin A; B-6; B-12; C; D; D2; D3; K)

Calories 152

41. Chia seeds bread

Ingredients:

3 cups of buckwheat flour

3 egg whites

1 cup of minced chia seeds

warm water

salt

½ pack of dry yeast

Preparation:

Mix flour, eggs and chia seeds with salt and yeast. Add warm water and stir until smooth dough. Let it stand in a warm place for about 30-40 minutes. Sprinkle with cold water and bake in preheated oven, at 350 degrees for about 40 minutes.

Nutritional values per 100g:

Carbohydrates 30g

Sugar 15.6g

Protein 23g

Total fat 16.4g

Sodium 183 mg

Potassium 319mg

Calcium 4.8mg

Iron 5.12mg

Vitamins (vitamin A; B-6; B-12; C; D; D2; D3; K; Riboflavin; Niacin; Thiamin; K)

Calories 309

42. Homemade peanut butter

Ingredients:

1 cup of peanuts, ground

3 tbsp of peanut oil

1 cup of Greek yogurt

¼ tsp of salt

Preparation:

Put all ingredients in a blender. This process takes about 30 seconds and your peanut butter is ready to eat!

Nutritional values per 100g:

Carbohydrates 21g

Sugar 17g

Protein 25g

Total fat 50.8g

Sodium 17mg

Potassium 622mg

Calcium 4.8mg

Iron 10.16mg

Vitamins (vitamin B-6; B-12; Riboflavin; Niacin; Thiamin; K)

Calories 580

43. Homemade vanilla cream

Ingredients:

1 cup of low fat cream

4 egg whites

1 tbsp of brown sugar

1 tsp of natural vanilla powder

1 tsp of vanilla extract

¼ tsp of cinnamon

Preparation:

Mix ingredients with a stick blender for few minutes. Leave in refrigerator overnight.

Nutritional values per 100g:

Carbohydrates 16g

Sugar 4.2g

Protein 19g

Total fat 8g

Sodium 56 mg

Potassium 122mg

Calcium 6.3mg

Iron 0.16mg

Vitamins (vitamin A; B;C; D; D2; D3)

Calories 136

44. Cherry ice cream

Ingredients:

½ cup of frozen cherries

½ cup of frozen yogurt

4 egg whites

¼ cup of almond milk

1 tsp of cherry extract

1 tbsp of brown sugar

1 tbsp of whipped dessert topping, fat free

Preparation:

Put cherries, egg whites, almond milk and sugar in a blender for 30 seconds, until you get a smooth mixture. Meanwhile, combine cherry extract with frozen yogurt and whipped dessert topping in a small bowl.

Pour both mixtures in tall glasses, so that the frozen yogurt is on top. Leave in the refrigerator overnight.

Nutritional values per 100g:

Carbohydrates 8g

Sugar 6.4g

Protein 15.6g

Total fat 6.8g

Sodium 132 mg

Potassium 121mg

Calcium 2.3mg

Iron 1.23mg

Vitamins (vitamin A; B-6; B-12; C; D; D2; D3)

Calories 176

45. Homemade protein cocoa drink

Ingredients:

1 cup of skim milk

½ cup of almond milk

4 egg whites

2 tsp of cocoa powder

2 tsp of brown sugar

1 tbsp of non-fat dessert topping

Preparation:

Combine the almond milk and skim milk. Bring it to the boiling point, over a medium temperature. Remove from heat and add cocoa powder, egg whites and sugar. Mix well and cook for another 3-4 minutes, on a very low temperature, stirring constantly.

Nutritional values per 1 cup:

Carbohydrates 30.5g

Sugar 26.7g

Protein 26g

Total fat 15.8g

Sodium 577 mg

Potassium 245mg

Calcium 9.8mg

Iron 7.8mg

Vitamins (vitamin B-6; B-12; D; D2)

Calories 322

46. Chia seeds pate

Ingredients:

½ cup of chia seeds powder

¼ cup of chia seeds

½ cup of cottage cheese

3-4 cloves of garlic

¼ cup of skim milk

1 tbsp of mustard

¼ tsp of salt

Preparation:

Chop the garlic and mix with mustard. In a large bowl, combine cottage cheese with skim milk, salt, chia seeds powder and chia seeds. Mix well and add garlic and mustard. Allow it to stand in the refrigerator for about an hour.

Nutritional values per 100g:

Carbohydrates 23g

Sugar 8.1g

Protein 24.2g

Total fat 10.6g

Sodium 177 mg

Potassium 312mg

Calcium 4.6mg

Iron 4.16mg

Vitamins (vitamin A; B-6; B-12; C; D; D2; D3; K; Riboflavin; Niacin; Thiamin; K)

Calories 174

47. Oatmeal with marple syrup

Ingredients:

1 cup of rolled oats

½ cup of strawberries

1 tsp of marple syrup

1 cup of Greek yogurt

1 tbsp of brown sugar

1 tbsp of honey

4 egg whites

Preparation:

Combine the oats with Greek yogurt in a large bowl. Wash and chop the strawberries into small pieces. Mix the strawberries with brown sugar and honey. Mash with a fork and add the oats. Top with marple syrup.

Nutritional values per 100g:

Carbohydrates 16.2g

Sugar 11 g

Protein 17.1 g

Total fat 9.8g

Sodium 168 mg

Potassium 289mg

Calcium 5.1mg

Iron 1.41mg

Vitamins (vitamin A; B-6; B-12; C; D; D2; D3; K; Riboflavin; Niacin; Thiamin; K)

Calories 118

48. Avocado and hazelnuts smoothie

Ingredients:

1 medium avocado

½ cup of hazelnuts, ground

3 egg whites

2 tbsp of honey

2 cups of skim milk

½ cup of ice cubes

fresh mint, few leaves

Preparation:

Cut the avocados in half, remove the pit and peel them. Then chop into small pieces, place in a blender, add milk, egg whites, hazelnuts, honey and ice cubes. Mix well for 30-40 seconds.

Nutritional values per one cup:

Carbohydrates 8.1g

Sugar 6.4g

Protein 21.7 g

Total fat 14.1g

Sodium 144 mg

Potassium 223mg

Calcium 4.81mg

Iron 2.21mg

Vitamins (vitamin A; B-6; B-12; C; D; D2; D3; K; Riboflavin; Niacin; Thiamin; K)

Calories 87

49. Creamy banana delight

Ingredients

1 glass of low fat yogurt

¼ cup of skim milk

1 tbsp of coconut flour

1 large banana

3 egg whites

2 tbsp of brown sugar

Preparation:

Make this smoothie by mixing banana, sugar, coconut flour, egg whites, yogurt and milk in a blender for 30-40 seconds.

Serve immediately!

Nutritional values per one cup:

Carbohydrates 7.2g

Sugar 6.1g

Protein 26.2 g

Total fat 10.2g

Sodium 123 mg

Potassium 224mg

Calcium 3.9mg

Iron 2.17mg

Vitamins (vitamin A; B-6; B-12; C; D; D2; D3; K; Riboflavin; Niacin; Thiamin; K)

Calories 85

50. Strawberry and chia yogurt

Ingredients:

1 cup of strawberry yogurt

½ cup of Greek yogurt

½ cup of non fat cream

3 egg whites

1 tbsp of strawberry extract

3 tbsp of brown sugar

Preparation:

Combine the ingredients in a blender for 30-40 seconds, until smooth mixture. Let it stand in the refrigerator for about an hour before serving.

Nutritional values per one cup:

Carbohydrates 9.2g

Sugar 6.1g

Protein 25.7 g

Total fat 9.2g

Sodium 134 mg

Potassium 226mg

Calcium 4.92mg

Iron 2.21mg

Vitamins (vitamin A; B-6; B-12; C; D; D2; D3; K; Riboflavin; Niacin; Thiamin; K)

Calories 87

51. Boiled eggs with chopped basil

Ingredients:

2 eggs

1 tsp of chopped basil

pepper

Preparation:

Boil eggs for 10 minutes. Peel and chop into small pieces. Sprinkle with chopped basil.

Nutritional values per 100 g:

Carbohydrates 1.1g

Sugar 0g

Protein 13g

Total fat (good monounsaturated fat) 11g

Sodium 124mg

Potassium 126mg

Calcium 50mg

Iron 1.2mg

Vitamins (vitamin A; B-6; B-12; C)

Calories 155

52. Mixed fruits and vegetables shake

Ingredients:

1 cup of mixed blueberries, raspberries, blackberries and strawberries

½ cup of chopped baby spinach

2 cups of water

Preparation:

Mix ingredients in a blender for few minutes.

Nutritional values for 1 cup:

Carbohydrates 9.2g

Sugar 6.15g

Protein 8.75g

Total fat 0.87g

Sodium 54.8mg

Potassium 107.8mg

Calcium 82mg

Iron 2.03mg

Vitamins (Vitamin C total ascorbic acid; B-6; B-12; Folate-DFE; A-RAE; A-IU; E-alpha-tocopherol; D; D-D2+D3; K-phylloquinone; Thianin; Riboflavin; Niacin)

Calories 42.6

Other Great Titles by This Author

www.ingramcontent.com/pod-product-compliance
Lightning Source LLC
Chambersburg PA
CBHW071742080526
44588CB00013B/2123